T 18576

THE ASANTE KINGDOM

At the height of its power, the influence of the Asante Kingdom extended beyond the borders of present-day Ghana.

~African Civilizations~

THE ASANTE KINGDOM

Carol Thompson

A First Book

Franklin Watts
A Division of Grolier Publishing
New York / London / Hong Kong / Sydney
Danbury, Connecticut

Cover photograph ©: Art Resource.

Photographs copyright ©: Trip/M. Jelliffe/The Viesti Collection, Inc.: pp. 7, 15, 31; Werner Forman Archive/British Museum: p. 9; Werner Forman Archive: pp. 13, 19, 23, 24; Herbert M. Cole: pp. 16, 35, 38, 40; Art Resource, NY: p. 27; Aldo Tutino/Art Resource, NY: p. 29; from Thomas Edward Bowdich's *Mission from Cape Coast to Ashantee*, 1819 (reprinted, London, 1966): p. 42; J. J. Foxx/NYC: p. 45; Courtesy of Jack Tilton Gallery, NY: p. 47; Colin Garratt, Milepost 92½/Corbis: p. 49; Ghana Information Service: p. 50; Hulton-Deutsch Collection/Corbis: p. 52; Dave Houser/Corbis: p. 55; Charles & Josette Lenars/Corbis: p. 56.

Library of Congress Cataloging-in-Publication Data

Thompson, Carol (Carol Ann)
    The Asante Kingdom / Carol Thompson. — 1st ed.
      p.   cm. — (African civilizations)
    Includes bibliographical references and index.
    Summary: Surveys the history and culture of the Asante Kingdom in West Africa, from its founding in the late seventeenth century to its clashes with the British and eventual decline in the nineteenth century.
    ISBN 0-531-20287-9
    1. Ashanti (African people)—History—Juvenile literature. 2. Ashanti (African people)—Social life and customs—Juvenile literature. [1. Ashanti (Kingdom)—History. 2. Ashanti (African people)]
    I. Title. II. Series.
DT507,T56   1998
966.7'018—dc21
                                 97-33079
                                     CIP
                                     AC

CONTENTS

INTRODUCTION

The Asante (ah-SAN-tee) Kingdom rose to power in the 1670s in the gold-rich forest region of what is now Ghana, West Africa. The founder of the kingdom and the first king of the Asante, or *asantehene* (ah-SUN-te-HEE-nee) was Osei Tutu (OH-say-too-too). He was assisted by the chief priest of the Asante, Okomfo Anokye (oh-KOM-foh-ah-NOHK-yeh), who was his best friend. Okomfo Anokye gave the Asante nation its most important symbol: the Golden Stool.

The Asante Kingdom grew by persuading neighboring states to join the Asante *Confederacy*, a union of states. The core of the Asante Confederacy was founded by people who lived within a 20-mile (32-km) radius of Kumasi (koo-MAH-see), the capital of the Asante region. The Asante

The current *asantehene*, Opoku Ware II, is seated beside the Golden Stool, which lies on its own chair. The Asante regard the Golden Stool as the resting place of the soul of the nation.

also conquered many surrounding states that did not join the confederacy voluntarily. Although these peoples lived in separate states, their languages and cultures were very similar. Together, these peoples are known as the Akan; they share a broadly similar culture and speak similar versions of the Twi language, but they have a history of rivalry.

As the Asante Kingdom absorbed neighboring states, it became ever more powerful and gained greater control of trade in the region. During the 1700s, at the height of its expansion, the influence of the Asante Kingdom extended beyond the borders of modern Ghana, making it the largest kingdom in West Africa at the time.

One of the Asante Kingdom's major goals was to defeat those Akan states to the south that controlled the coast of the Atlantic Ocean, where trade was conducted with Europeans. The coastal states acted as *middlemen* in the trade between the interior and the coast, keeping much of the profits for themselves. Only by conquering these states could the Asante eliminate the middlemen, trade directly with the Europeans, and receive greater profit. Although the Asante did gain some access to the coast, they were unable to control trade completely. Their greatest rivals were the Fante.

At first the Asante Kingdom's main export was gold, but before long the slave trade became more important than gold. Nearly 700,000 enslaved people were taken from the region of modern Ghana during the eighteenth century and sent mostly to the Americas. Through middlemen, the Asante traded with Europeans for metal, cloth,

The Asante Kingdom became famous as a gold exporter. These beautiful gold ornaments were worn as badges by some of the Asante Kingdom's officials.

firearms, liquor, luxury goods, and other items. The kingdom also supplied kola nuts to African peoples in the north in return for cotton, leather, and metal goods.

In the early nineteenth century Great Britain and other nations outlawed the slave trade. After having bought enslaved Africans from the Asante for centuries, they tried to stop the Asante from raiding and enslaving their neighbors.

The British, who had allied themselves with the Fante, hoped to conquer the Asante and gain control of their gold. Eventually, after many wars and fierce Asante resistance, the British did defeat the Asante Kingdom, which then came under British authority.

Together with other British-held territory in the region, Asante territory became part of the British colony of Gold Coast in 1902. At that time and throughout the colonial era the Asante were known as the Ashanti.

The Asante played a leading role in encouraging the people of the Gold Coast to resist British control and demand independence. Finally, in 1957, Britain granted independence to the Gold Coast. It was the first of all the European colonies in Africa to become independent.

The people of the Gold Coast changed its name to Ghana after independence. This name honored the Empire of Ghana, a powerful gold-producing kingdom that had flourished in West Africa from about 750 to 1076, many centuries before the Asante had built their own kingdom on the trading of gold.

AKAN CULTURE AND A NEW KINGDOM

Centuries before the founding of the Asante Kingdom, separate Akan peoples in the gold-rich forest zone began to establish small kingdoms or states. The first of these kingdoms included Bono Manso, Akwamu, Adanse, Twifo, Sefwi, Wasaw, Akyem, Fante, and especially Denkyira, which had become the most powerful state in the region by 1650.

THE ECONOMY

Scholars believe that the Akan peoples learned the skills of metal-working and weaving from people to the north in about the fourteenth century. This new technology and increasing trade were two of the main factors that encouraged the development of Akan states.

Farming improved as iron for tools became more available—first through a steady increase in local production and later through trade with Europeans, who first visited the Atlantic coast of present-day Ghana in the late 1400s. Larger harvests supported larger populations and further stimulated trade, because surpluses could be sold to other communities.

The main crop of the Akan forest region was the yam, which was probably first cultivated there. Later, Europeans introduced new crops, including corn, cassava, coco-yam, peanuts, oranges, avocados, tomatoes, and pineapples.

For many centuries before the founding of the Asante Kingdom, gold had been mined in West Africa south of the Sahara Desert. Gold was the basis of long-distance trade between Africans and the Muslim world, which used gold as currency. Some scholars believe that the Akan were drawn into this West African network of gold trading by the fourteenth century. They panned gold from the rivers in the region and sold gold dust and nuggets to African

The yam was once the main crop of the Akan forest region. Nana Owusu Sampa III, the ruler of the Akan state of Akrokerri, parades in the street during the annual Yam Festival, which is an important celebration among the Asante.

traders who, in turn, sold it for export to Arab countries. Gold dust eventually became the Asante *currency*.

SOCIETY AND RELIGION

In the Akan region all land was organized into states. *Oman* is the Asante word for state. Each *oman* had its own ruler, or *omanhene*. He ruled over a *hierarchy* of chiefs, subchiefs, councils of elders, priests, artisans, and young men's groups.

Today—as in the past—the basis of Akan society is the family. In several Akan groups, including the Asante, the mother's family line is of particular importance. It is through the blood of the mother that people trace their descent. Among the Asante, a person inherits according to the mother's family line, known as the *abasua*.

The family does not consist only of the living. The Asante and other Akan peoples consider their ancestors vital and ever-present members of the family. It is believed that the ancestors will protect the family if their living relatives pay them proper respect by remembering and honoring them. The worlds of the living and the dead are thus closely connected.

The Akan peoples honor especially influential ancestors with portrait sculptures called *akya'mma*, made of baked clay, or terra-cotta. These sculptures are not placed in the burial ground but nearby in a grove for ancestral spirits called *asamanpow*, or "place of pots." There, in the sacred grove, individuals make offerings and appeals to their ancestors.

Asante priests help their communities honor the spiritual powers, such as ancestral spirits and nature spirits. This diviner is attached to the *asantehene*'s court in the capital of the Asante Kingdom, Kumasi.

Asante stool decorated with silver plates, with bells attached on either side

The Akan consider land sacred because it is associated both with ancestors and with nature spirits, which are believed to live in rivers, rocks, and other natural features. This means that the economy and the politics of the Asante were closely connected to Akan religious beliefs. The political unit of an Asante village or state was defined by an area of territory, which in turn was closely connected to the ancestors and spirits.

STOOLS

Wooden stools are perhaps the most important objects in Asante daily life. The Asante believe that a person's soul lives in his or her stool. The stool is therefore a very personal object, and it is generally used only by its owner. It is turned on its side when not being used as a seat.

Upon the death of a prominent person, such as an elder, priest, chief, military officer, or queen mother, his or her stool is blackened with ashes and other substances. It is then placed in a special stool room along with those of other important members of the community. The stool room is cared for by the village chief (*odekuro*) and elders.

OSEI TUTU AND THE GOLDEN STOOL

When Osei Tutu was born in 1660, the Asante *oman,* or state, was made up of seven chiefdoms that were loosely allied but were rivals. The Asante state was in turn ruled by the powerful state of Denkyira (DEN-ke-rah) to the south. Denkyira and the nearby Fante state both controlled trade with the Europeans and became very wealthy.

The Denkyira people had attacked the Asante with weapons obtained from the Europeans and had enslaved them. The Asante were forced to pay *tribute* to the Denkyira. This tax of goods acknowledged the authority of Denkyira over the Asante state.

When Osei Tutu was young, the leader of the small Asante state was his great-uncle, Obiri Yeboa. Obiri Yeboa sent the young prince Osei Tutu to the court of Boa Amponsem, the ruler of Denkyira. Perhaps Boa Amponsem had demanded this as a way of ensuring the loyalty of the Asante, who would have been unlikely to rebel while their prince was living at the ruler's court. Or perhaps Obiri Yeboa sent his son there to learn the secrets of Denkyira's success.

In Denkyira, Osei Tutu studied Akan law and customs and learned diplomacy. The event that most influenced his future, however, was meeting the powerful priest Okomfo Anokye, who became his best friend. Okomfo Anokye was famous for his rain-making ability and other magical powers.

When Obiri Yeboa died, Osei Tutu returned to Kumasi with Okomfo Anokye as his companion and adviser. Together they decided to stage an event that would bind the seven chiefdoms of the Asante people more strongly together. A great meeting was called under the sacred *kuma* tree that stood at the

Stools and chairs belonging to chiefs are still carried to important public events.

center of Kumasi's market and for which the capital had been named. Messengers spread the news throughout the region that each of the seven chiefs was to bring his sacred stool to the meeting, held on a Friday, and that Okomfo Anokye would appoint a new ruler of all the Asante.

When the chiefs gathered, they placed their stools in the center of the meeting place. Okomfo Anokye began to dance and entered into a *trance*, during which he communicated with Nyankopon, the Supreme Being. Nyankopon sent a bolt of lightning that *consumed* the seven stools of the Asante chiefs, covering the area with a dark cloud of smoke. When the smoke cleared, a blackened stool had descended from the sky to rest on the knees of Osei Tutu. As the crowd watched, the blackened stool turned to gold.

Okomfo Anokye explained to the people that Nyankopon had clearly shown through these magical events that the seven Asante groups should cease their conflicts and be united as one nation ruled by Osei Tutu. The Sika Dwa Kofi, "the Golden Stool created on Friday," was the symbol of the new nation. Just as the stools of living people and of the dead were the resting places for their souls, so too the Golden Stool contained the *sumsum*, or soul, of the Asante nation. The Golden Stool was far more spiritually powerful than any other stool. Nobody—not even the king—would ever sit on it, because nobody had the right to oppress the Asante nation or regard himself or herself as superior to it.

These events, which occurred sometime in the 1670s, gave the Asante a new unity. The seven chiefs all swore loyalty to Osei Tutu, who took the title *asantehene*, king of the Asante. The people of the kingdom were urged to forget previous traditions and place their loyalties with the Golden Stool. Allegiance to it guaranteed their wealth and welfare. So long as the peoples of the Asante Kingdom acted as allies, the safety and prosperity of the kingdom were assured.

Osei Tutu received tribute and military support from each of the chiefs and created new laws that applied to everybody in the Asante Kingdom. The united kingdom was immediately richer and more powerful than it had been as a loose alliance of rival chiefs. Soon it would become a powerful state and a rival of Denkyira.

ASANTE ROYAL ART

The *asantehene* controlled the use, sale, and taxation of gold, which was a major source of the Asante Kingdom's wealth. Gold was also *conspicuous* in the court, where the royal family and important officials wore special items of dress, or *regalia*, given to them by the king. These included gold jewelry and gold-leaf-covered swords, staffs, headdresses, tunics, sandals, and other items.

Thomas Edward Bowdich, a British official who visited the Asante Kingdom in 1817, described the spectacle of the *asantehene*'s royal court. He saw gold ornaments and gold and silver pipes and canes dazzling the eye in every direction. Swords

An attendant to an *omanhene*, or head of an Akan state, wearing ceremonial regalia

were adorned with the heads of rams and other animals "as large as life, cast in gold."

REGALIA
Some items of regalia were reserved for certain types of officials. Sword-bearers, for example, served as

Asante spokesman wearing kente cloth and holding his staff of office. The carvings atop spokesmen's staffs, which are covered in gold leaf, refer to well-known Asante proverbs.

the king's ambassadors, messengers, and escorts for visitors to the kingdom.

The counselors and spokesmen of Akan chiefs still carry staffs topped with gold-covered sculptures that refer to well-known Akan proverbs. A sculpture of a man holding an egg, for example, refers to the proverb that power is like an egg—if it is not held carefully it can easily fall from one's grasp and, if held too tightly, it will be crushed. Spokesmen address the people on behalf of chiefs. These skilled public speakers use their staffs to help make points.

THE CONTROL OF GOLD

The Asante gold reserve was called the Adaka Kese, or Great Chest. Nearly 7 feet (2 m) long and 4 feet (1.3 m) wide, it contained about 25,000 pounds (11,340 kg) of gold dust and nuggets, worth about $160 million today. The *gyaasewahene*, or head of the king's *civil service*, was the guardian of the Great Chest and held the only key to the room where it was kept.

The Asante used a balance scale with brass counterweights to measure quantities of gold dust. An English trader who visited the coast of West Africa in 1553 wrote:

"These people are very wary in their bargaining, and will not lose count of a single spark of the gold they offer for sale. They use their own weights and measures, and they are very careful about how they use them. Anyone who wants to deal with them must do so decently, for they will not trade if they are badly treated."

The *asantehene*, however, could afford to be lavish with gold dust. Visitors to the kingdom in the eighteenth century described how Asantehene Opoku Ware's servants oiled the king's skin and hair and powdered him completely with fine gold dust twice a day. Only then was he ready to appear in public.

The goldsmiths of Kumasi were controlled by the king. Senior chiefs had to obtain the permission of the *asantehene* before they could *commission* gold ornaments from these highly skilled craftsmen. A 1909 colonial survey showed that eighty-five goldsmiths worked in or near Kumasi. They accompanied Asante armies into battle in order to make the portrait sculptures of slain enemies. These portraits were used to adorn Asante stools and swords.

COUNTERWEIGHTS
Brass counterweights for gold trading are a distinctive Asante art form, and they are popular with col-

An Asante brass counterweight in the form of a rider

lectors. Centuries-old weights have abstract geometric shapes. Later examples are in the form of people, plants, animals, objects, or scenes of daily life. Often these images—usually no more than 2.5 inches (6 cm) high or wide—relate to proverbs. A weight showing a leopard with a gun in its mouth standing over a hunter, for example, refers to the proverb "Think before you act." Though tiny, the weights contain great meaning, and they provide windows into Asante life.

Traders and the treasuries of Akan states had their own sets of weights. Chiefs brought out the state's weights—which were very heavy and used for measuring large quantities of gold—on important occasions, such as wars, large celebrations, and royal funerals. They were evidence of the wealth and power of the state.

Counterweights and other Asante metal objects were cast using the lost-wax process. Artists first form an object in wax and then encase it in a clay mold. The completed mold is heated until the clay hardens and the wax melts. The liquid wax is poured out, and molten metal is poured into the cavity. When the metal has hardened, the baked clay shell is broken away to reveal the metal sculpture inside. This is then polished to a fine finish.

CLOTH

The *asantehene* also regulated the use of some cloth. Kente cloth, now famous worldwide, was invented in the 1600s and became the Asante royal cloth. Complex patterns were woven into narrow strips, which were then sewn together to form a large piece of cloth.

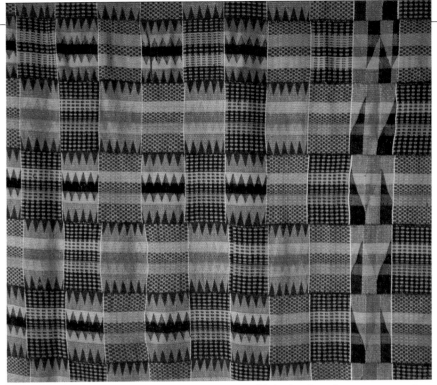

Kente cloth consists of several long strips of woven fabric that have been sewn together. This piece of cloth, which is approximately 11 x 8 feet (3.5 x 2.5 m), was woven from silk.

When European cloth entered the kingdom in the 1700s, the *asantehene* ordered the finest fabrics, including Chinese silks, to be unraveled and rewoven into Asante-style cloth for his personal use.

The Asante and other Akan peoples also still use *adinkra*, which is cotton cloth stamped with symbolic black designs. *Adinkra* made with a bright or light-colored background is used for festive or daily wear; red cloths or dark cloths are used for mourning.

SHADE

For the Asante, shade was associated with power. Every chief was expected to plant a new shade tree when he took power, decorate the shade trees of his predecessors with white cloth, and vow to rule well and guard his people. Before going to war, a chief vowed to his people that their enemy would not be allowed to enter the city and cut down the tree he had planted. After each war, new trees were planted. When a chief died it was said that "a great tree has fallen." Trees like the sacred *kuma* of Kumasi were regarded as signs of a city's physical and spiritual well-being.

Umbrellas played a similar role. Asante chiefs appeared in public under huge umbrellas that were associated with shade trees and were said to provide both physical coolness and spiritual coolness, or calm. They are still used on state occasions.

By the seventeenth century, great multicolored umbrellas were in use in the Asante Kingdom—perhaps in imitation of the fourteenth-century Kingdom of Mali, where the king was shaded by a silk umbrella topped by a gold sculpture of a bird. The watercolors illustrating Bowdich's account of

Among the Asante, trees and umbrellas are associated with physical and spiritual well-being.

his visit to the Asante Kingdom in 1817 show many such umbrellas used by chiefs. Also seen are *palanquins*, large hammock-like thrones for carrying chiefs, kings, and members of the royal family.

THE EXPANSION OF THE ASANTE KINGDOM

Osei Tutu was a wise ruler who used many strategies to unify and expand the Asante Kingdom that he had founded. He created a constitution, made Kumasi the kingdom's capital, and established a state celebration in Kumasi called the Odwira festival, which all members of the Asante Confederacy were required to attend. This festival was designed to encourage a sense of peace and solidarity throughout the kingdom.

At the same time, Osei Tutu built a nearly invincible army. Neighboring peoples were persuaded, threatened, or forced by military defeat to join the Asante Confederacy. Osei Tutu led a series of political campaigns to expand the kingdom's territory. In 1701, the Asante at last defeated the kingdom of Denkyira, which had so long oppressed them.

Osei Tutu was killed in battle in 1717 and was succeeded by his nephew Opoku Ware (oh-POK-oo-WAH-ray), who ruled as *asantehene* until his death in 1750.

OPOKU WARE

Opoku Ware, a great general, transformed the Asante Kingdom into the greatest power in the Akan region. He defeated the Akan states of Tekyiman in 1722–23 and Akyem in 1742, and he received *tribute* from other groups not fully incorporated into the Asante Confederacy. The influence of the kingdom extended well beyond the borders of modern Ghana.

Throughout this period of expansion, new villages and towns sprang up quickly, since Asante houses—made of wood and clay and roofed with palm fronds—are quick to build. Villages were linked with paths hacked through the dense forest. Over time these paths were enlarged into roads that linked villages to Kumasi. As the Asante state grew, Kumasi, which remains the capital of the Asante region to this day, became larger and more prosperous. Like spokes of a wheel, roads radiated outward from Kumasi to all areas of Asante control and influence. They were vital for long-distance trade and the travel of royal officials and messengers.

TRADE

During Osei Tutu's and Opoku Ware's reigns the Asante traded extensively with peoples to the north and with the Europeans who were established in forts along the coast to the south.

The first Europeans to sail to West Africa and begin trading on the coast were the Portuguese. In 1482 they were granted permission by the local Akan chiefs to build the fort of Elmina, which means "the mine," on the coast, where it stands today. At first the Portuguese traded metals—particularly brass and copper—for gold, ivory, and other African goods. They were delighted to have established direct contact with the gold-producing areas of West Africa. Up to that time Europe had been obliged to obtain most of its gold from Muslim traders who had carried the African gold north across the Sahara Desert.

The Portuguese fort, Elmina Castle

The Portuguese were also the first to transport enslaved Africans to Europe, where it rapidly became fashionable among the wealthy to have slaves in one's household. By 1550 the number of enslaved Africans in the Portuguese capital of Lisbon had reached 10 percent of the population.

The Portuguese already had an established system of plantations worked by slaves who were mostly Slavs, whose name was the origin of the word "slave." This system operated in Portugal, on Portuguese-controlled islands in the Mediterranean Sea, and on the island of São Tomé, in the Gulf of Guinea. After Europeans explored the Americas, this system was imposed there too. In 1532 enslaved Africans were first transported across the Atlantic to the Americas, where the Portuguese and the Spanish had established many plantations and mines.

Gold from the Americas also reduced the need for gold from Africa. Gradually Africa became more important to Portugal and other European nations as a source of slaves and of products such as ivory, rather than of gold. Enslaved Africans were taken from several parts of the West African coast, from present-day Senegal in the west to Angola in the south. The Guinea coast, in the region of what is now Ghana, was an important center for this terrible trade in enslaved humans.

THE ASANTE KINGDOM AND THE DUTCH

Even though the Asante enjoyed European products, they were wary of the Europeans and seldom dealt with them directly. By the reigns of Osei Tutu and Opoku Ware, the power of the Portuguese on the coast had greatly declined. The Dutch had taken over Elmina Castle, and the British had established a fort at Cape Coast.

By the time of Opoku Ware's death in 1750, the

Asante Kingdom controlled all of the region's major trade routes from the interior to the sea. Opoku Ware had even managed to collect rent from the new Dutch owners of Elmina Castle, which was the most important European trading fort in all of West Africa. The Dutch regarded the Asante as their main African trading partner. Two interesting examples illustrate the relationship between the Netherlands and the Asante Kingdom: Asantehene Opoku Ware ordered a coffin from Holland, and in 1826 the Asante presented the Dutch with a special Asante cloth that had the Dutch coat of arms printed in the center.

EXPANSION

Through trade with the Dutch and other Europeans, the Asante obtained firearms that enabled them to conquer their enemies and neighboring peoples whom they had never before dared to attack. They sold their captives into slavery. The Asante also used slaves to mine gold in order to meet the demand for gold of the Europeans. Instead of panning for gold in the rivers, slaves were now forced to dig and work mines.

In the eighteenth century the Asante obtained powerful firearms in their trade with Europeans. This hunter's costume is ceremonial. The charms that cover it provide spiritual protection, enhancing luck in hunting and success in war.

In 1744–45, Asante soldiers armed with firearms easily defeated the cavalry of Dagomba, a northern state in whose open country the Asante had never before been prepared to fight. The Asante held Dagomba as a tributary state for nearly one hundred years. By the mid-eighteenth century the Asante had also taken control of the cotton-producing city of

Salaga, inhabited by the neighboring Gonja people.

The eighteenth century was a period of expansion for the Asante. But in 1750 the Baule people—an Akan group—broke away from the Asante Confederacy and founded a new state farther west in what is now Côte d'Ivoire (Ivory Coast).

OSEI KWADWO

Osei Kwadwo (OH-say-KWA-dwo), who reigned from 1764 to 1777, introduced changes that increased the authority of the central government in Kumasi and expanded the king's civil service. Bureaucrats were appointed according to their abilities rather than because they were from chiefly families. Hard-working persons from throughout the Confederacy were rewarded with important posts in business and politics, which increased national unity and loyalty to the capital.

Osei Kwadwo paid special attention to the administration of trade. He appointed officials to control it from Kumasi and created a treasury to run the finances of the kingdom. The treasury was staffed by Muslims, whose skills in mathematics and writing in Arabic were of particular use to the

Osei Kwadwo employed Muslims in the civil service to keep records in Arabic. Today, children in many West African countries write their lessons in Arabic on washable wooden boards.

asantehene, since the Asante did not then have a tradition of writing. For centuries the Asante used spoken words rather than written records to remember the past. Today Asante knowledge and tradition are maintained and passed on both in written form and as oral history—in proverbs, stories, song and dance, and visually through works of art.

During Osei Kwadwo's reign, tension increased between the Asante and the Fante. In 1765, they had a military clash. From that time forward they had periodic conflicts, even after Osei Kwadwo's death.

4 THE ASANTE AND THE BRITISH

Osei Bonsu, who reigned from 1779 to 1824, was the last *asantehene* to enjoy full control of the Asante Kingdom.

In 1805 the Asante attacked the British fort at Abora, where several Fante soldiers had taken refuge. Neither the Fante nor the British put up much of a fight. The Asante defeated the Fante and were acknowledged as the rulers of the coast.

In 1806, the Fante killed an Asante diplomatic group accompanied by a sword-bearer and seized the royal golden sword. The incident caused the Asante to invade the Fante region. After a long conflict the Asante eventually retreated.

This illustration was published in Bowdich's account of his visit to the Asante capital in 1817.

In 1807 the British outlawed slavery, as the Danes had done five years earlier. This removed one of the most profitable trading activities of the Asante and one of the cornerstones of their relationship with Europeans. The British protected the Fante and the Ga, another coastal people, from the Asante, but the Asante refused to halt their military and slaving activities.

INCREASING CONTACT WITH EUROPEANS

Gradually, the Asante—particularly their leaders— came into more direct contact with the Europeans.

For their own use they imported such goods as cloth, liquor, silver vessels, clothing, flags, gold-topped canes, elaborate hats, carriages, magic lanterns, lathes, and leather shoes.

Between 1817 and 1820, European agents, such as Bowdich, were allowed to enter Kumasi for the first time. Bowdich and others later wrote about their favorable impressions of the beautiful, clean, and comfortable city of about 40,000 residents. They reported that all of Kumasi's major streets and its seventy-seven neighborhoods were named. The main street, over 328 feet (100 m) wide, was used for major receptions and parades.

Another sign of the kingdom's increased open-ness was the number of foreigners employed by the *asantehene* during Osei Bonsu's reign. For the first time Europeans were allowed in the civil service. In fact, a few decades later, in 1875, a Frenchman named Marie-Joseph Bonnat was appointed co-governor of a province by the *asantehene*. Bonnat described how the king in Kumasi "knows each day what is happening in the most humble villages of his empire. From all sides he receives reports and minute details . . . day and night, the orders of the king are despatched in all directions." To ensure the safety of the Confederacy and guard against revolts by lesser chiefs, the *asantehene* had a special security force in Kumasi called the Ankobia.

Asante military power—fed by the regular exchange of gold dust for guns from the Dutch at Elmina—kept the British and their Fante allies in a state of constant military alert, and even prevented the Fante from farming. Although the Asante had conquered them, the Fante were never fully absorbed into the Asante Confederacy. They retained their independence, and their armies were never disbanded.

OSEI BONSU'S NATIONAL PROJECTS

To celebrate his victories, Osei Bonsu initiated many building projects to improve the capital and its roads. According to Bowdich, army captains returning from war were rewarded with large sums of gold from the royal treasury to decorate or enlarge their houses.

For himself, Osei Bonsu erected the great Stone Palace, modeled after the Europeans' coastal forts. The building, decorated with gold,

Horns and drums used by the *asantehene's* orchestra were once kept in sheds at the Stone Palace. Today, too, Akan rulers have court musicians, such as these horn players.

ivory, and brass, was completed in 1822. It was mainly used as a treasure storehouse, especially for precious items from overseas. Decades later, in 1874, British soldiers and journalists described the Stone Palace: "It had a courtyard, under the sheds of which the king kept his cellar of palm wine—of champagne and brandy too, they say— his umbrellas new and old, his chairs and palanquins covered with scarlet and leopard skin." Also stored in the sheds were the horns and drums used by the royal orchestra. On the upper floors of the Stone Palace were "the art treasures of the monarchy," including the *asantehene*'s collection of books in various languages, paintings, engravings, carpets, glass, silver, clocks, and fine furniture.

CONFLICT WITH THE BRITISH

During the last half of the nineteenth century the Asante struggled to balance opposing social and political forces. Their demand for profit and power made them reliant on war and conquest, yet trade demanded peace.

The powers of the European trading nations and their relationships with the Akan states shifted considerably after 1850, when the Danish left their coastal African forts. By 1872, the Dutch had also left, leaving the British as the sole European coastal power. The Asante seized control of nearly all these coastal states between 1869 and 1872. Meanwhile, the British tightened their control of the coastal region south of Asante territory by making it a British colony, the Gold Coast Colony, in 1874.

Having proclaimed their authority over part of the coastal region, the British began to push the Asante inland. This caused the war of 1874. The

This sculpture by David Hammons, "Tree of Hope," expresses the despair felt by some African-Americans today. It provides a visual parallel to the Asante experience when the British cut down the sacred *kuma*.

British entered Kumasi and destroyed part of it. They looted and dynamited the Stone Palace. They also cut down Kumasi's sacred *kuma*. Furthermore, they demanded that the Asante pay the British 50,000 ounces of gold (to pay for the cost of the British military expedition); accept the presence of a British official to be stationed in Kumasi; and surrender the Golden Stool. The Asante refused.

The unreasonable British demands remained a source of tension between the British and the Asante.

5 ASANTE RESISTANCE

After the war of 1874, the Asante Kingdom unwillingly became a British Protectorate. British companies started mining gold in Adanse and the southern Asante region. In 1896 the British military occupied Kumasi and established a British fort.

The last decades of the nineteenth century were a very difficult and unhappy time for the people of the Asante Kingdom. Several *asantehene*s were removed by the British or died. Nonetheless, the Asante maintained a spirit of resistance.

In 1894, Agyeman Prempeh was enthroned *asantehene*. One of his advisers was the chief of Edweso state, Afrane Kuma.

After they defeated the Asante, the British opened gold mines in Asante territory. Today, gold mining continues in Ghana.

When Prempeh I became *asantahene*, he was forced to accept the permanent stationing of a British official in Kumasi. He refused, however, to pay for the costs of the 1874 British military expedition or to surrender the sacred Golden Stool. He was arrested by the British in 1896. They exiled him to the Seychelles Islands along with many of his advisers, including Afrane Kuma. In the absence of Afrane Kuma, his mother, Yaa Asantewa, stepped in to rule Edweso state. She became an important political leader among the Asante.

Queen Yaa Asantewa is an Asante heroine. She led her people with a spirit of fierce resistance into war against the British. Above she is shown in battle gear, although this was probably posed for a photographer.

YAA ASANTEWA

On March 25, 1900, the governor of the Gold Coast, Sir Frederick Hodgson, paid his first official visit to Kumasi. His private secretary described how during celebrations Yaa Asantewa, now queen of the Asante, "caused much excitement by carefully examining the Governor's medals," thereby mocking British authority.

The Governor complained that the earlier expedition costs had still not been paid and that the Golden Stool had not been surrendered. He demanded that it be brought out so that he could sit on it. This outraged the Asante, who would have burned the stool that held their national soul rather than surrender it. In turn, they demanded the return of their king, which Governor Hodgson could not guarantee. Led by Yaa Asantewa, the Asante chiefs decided on war. They summoned their armies.

Meanwhile, Hodgson had sent out troops to search for the Golden Stool. They returned empty-handed, reporting unrest in the countryside. Sensing danger, Hodgson tried to negotiate with the Asante leaders in Kumasi. He desperately

British illustration of a battle during the war between the Asante and the British in 1900

telegraphed for reinforcements—until the Asante cut the wire. By April 25, Kumasi was surrounded by Asante armies. The Governor, other British officials, and their African allies and captives were trapped in the British fort, short of food and ammunition.

The most powerful British ally, the king of the state of Bekwai, was too fearful of Yaa Asantewa to send his army to assist the British. He could hardly restrain his men from joining Yaa Asantewa's side.

After two months, the Governor and some officers made a desperate escape to Cape Coast, leaving only 153 men defending the fort. The Asante made only small attacks on them. In the meantime, the British rushed 1,400 troops from other parts of Africa to suppress the Asante, now between 40,000 and 50,000 strong.

With superior weapons and after a three-month campaign, the British defeated the Asante. Queen Yaa Asantewa held out to the very end. She was finally captured in 1900 and exiled to Seychelles. She died in 1921.

After the war that Yaa Asantewa inspired, the British treated the Asante with far greater respect. To this day the Asante still sing of their great leader: "Yaa Asantewa, the warrior woman who carries a gun and a sword of state in battle."

THE ASANTE LEGACY

After the British defeated the Asante in 1900, the Golden Stool was secretly buried, hidden away until 1921. A few years later, in 1924, the British released Prempeh I from exile. He agreed to rule as king of the Asante but to recognize the authority of the British over the Gold Coast. By 1902, Asante territory had officially become a colony of the British Empire.

In 1933, the Asante Confederacy was restored. Two years later, in 1935, Prempeh II was enthroned, and the Golden Stool was displayed in public for the first time since 1896. This demonstrated that the Asante had, throughout this period

Opoku Ware II was enthroned *asantehene* in 1970.

Asante art traditions still followed today are part of the rich legacy of the Asante Kingdom.

of resistance, preserved its soul. The current *asantehene*, Opoku Ware II, who succeeded Prempeh II in 1970, has also appeared in public with the Golden Stool.

The Asante spirit of resistance inspired all the people of the Gold Coast colony—and Britain's other African colonies—to work toward independence from Britain. The Asante remain an influential group in the modern state of Ghana, which is also a member of the British Commonwealth.

Kente cloth, while still hand-woven in Ghana, is now also factory-printed on baseball caps, umbrellas, and many other items throughout the world. It is a sign of the rich legacy of the Asante, and a powerful symbol of African identity.

TIMELINE

c. A.D. 1500	Adanse and Akwamu, early Akan states, emerge
c. 1680–1717	Kumasi emerges as capital of the new Asante Kingdom; Osei Tutu reigns in the Gold Coast region
1717	Opoku Ware becomes *asantehene*
1742	Opoku Ware defeats Akyem, making the Asante the most powerful kingdom along the Gold Coast
1744–45	Gonja and Dagomba become Asante tributary states
1750	Opoku Ware dies; Kusi Obodu becomes *asantehene*; Asante civil war
1764	Osei Kwadwo becomes *asantehene*
1765	Coastal states form an alliance against the Asante
1777	Osei Kwadwo dies; Osei Kwame becomes *asantehene*
1779	Osei Bonsu becomes *asantehene*
1802	Denmark is first slaving nation to outlaw slave trade
1806–07	Asante invade Fante territory but eventually retreat
1807	Great Britain and the United States outlaw slave trade
1817	English expedition arrives in Kumasi to negotiate trade relations with Osei Bonsu
1823	Asante attack Denkyira, Wassa, Fante, and the British
1824	Osei Bonsu dies; last *asantehene* to have full control of Asante Kingdom

1874	War of 1874; Asante are defeated; Asantehene Kofi Kakari deposed by the British; Mensa Bonsu elected *asantehene*
1883	Asantehene Mensa Bonsu deposed by British; anarchy follows
1884	Kwaku Dua II becomes *asantehene*; he dies of smallpox
1894	Agyeman Prempeh becomes *asantehene*; Asante delegation leaves for England to protest British policy; delegation is not received
1896	British occupy Kumasi; Asantehene Prempeh I and advisers exiled to the Seychelles Islands; British proclaim a protectorate over Asante territory
1900	British demand Golden Stool; Queen Yaa Asantewa and Asante chiefs declare war against the British; the Asante are defeated
1902	Asante territory becomes British Gold Coast colony
1921	Yaa Asantewa dies
1924	Prempeh I returns to Kumasi from exile
1935	Prempeh II installed as Asantehene Osei Agyman Otumfo
1954	National Liberation Movement (NLM) of Gold Coast colony is founded
1957	Gold Coast colony becomes the independent nation of Ghana within the British Commonwealth

GLOSSARY

abasua descent of a family through the mother's line

asantehene king of the Asante

civil service administrative agency of government that is separate from the military

commission to order something to be made

confederacy alliance of several states for mutual support

conspicuous highly visible

consume to burn up, use up, eat, or drink

currency the form of money used in a society

gyaasewahene head of the Asante civil service

hierarchy system that involves ranking people according to their economic, social, or professional standing

kuma sacred tree in Kumasi

middleman agent or dealer who arranges business dealings between the producer of goods and the buyer of goods

palanquin throne-like chair supported on poles and carried by four people

regalia emblems or decorations of royalty or high rank

sumsum soul of a nation

trance state of semi-unconsciousness, as in hypnosis

tribute money or goods paid by a people or a state to a more powerful state

FOR FURTHER READING

Boateng, Faustine Ama. *Asante*. New York: Rosen Publishing Group, 1996.

Hintz, Martin. *Ghana*. Chicago: Children's Press, 1987.

Kellner, Doug. *Kwame Nkrumah*. Broomall, PA: Chelsea House, 1987.

FOR ADVANCED READERS

Cole, Herbert, and Doran Ross. *The Arts of Ghana*. Los Angeles: UCLA Press, 1977.

Davidson, Basil. *Africa in History*. New York: Macmillan, 1991.

McLeod, M. D. *The Asante*. London: British Museum Publications, 1981.

WEB SITES

Due to the changeable nature of the Internet, sites appear and disappear very quickly. Internet addresses must be entered with capital and lowercase letters exactly as they appear.

Africa Online: http://www.africaonline.com/AfricaOnline/coverkids.html

Baobab Project: http://web-dubois.fas.harvard.edu/dubois/baobab/

Women of Power: http://www.rust.net/~khnum/wmanit.htm

INDEX

ABOUT THE AUTHOR

Carol Thompson received a master's degree in art history from the University of Iowa in 1988. From 1987 to 1996 she was Curator for Education and Associate Curator at the Museum for African Art in New York City. Thompson has taught at New York University, the Fashion Institute of Technology, Pace University, and City College of New York. She is a frequent public speaker on the art and culture of Africa and the African diaspora, past and present. Her interest in African art has taken her to Burkina Faso, Ghana, Malawi, Mali, and Togo. She is currently completing a Ph.D. in Performance Studies at New York University's Tisch School of the Arts and teaching at Vassar College, New York University, and Drew University.